WHITNEY HOUSTON

TAKING PART

JEFF
SAVAGE

DILLON PRESS
Parsippany, New Jersey

Photo Credits
Front cover: Ipol, Inc./UPPA.
Back cover: Archive Photos/Reuters/Ed Carreon.

AP/Wide World Photos: 32, 38, 42; J. Scott Applewhite: 57; David Cohen: 30;
Benny Gool: 51; Chris O'Meara: 39; Andrew Savulich: 46; Kathy Willens: 58. Archive
Photos/Reuters/Jeff Christiansen: 55. Corbis-LGI Collection: 17; Neil Calandra: 9;
Karl A. Gehring: 64; Dave Hogan: 1, 19. Globe Photos, Inc.: 61; John Barrett: 20;
Walter Iooss, Jr.: 13. Supplied by Ipol, Inc./Warner Brothers: 3, 4, 7; Phil Roach: 10,
26, 35. New Jersey Newsphotos: 15, 22. Retna, Ltd./Larry Busacca: 37; Steve
Granitz: 59; Neal Preston: 45. Jack Vartoogian: 21. Courtesy, Walt Disney Company,
Touchstone Pictures, & the Samuel Goldwyn Company, photo by David Lee: 54.

Library of Congress Cataloging-in-Publication Data
Savage, Jeff, 1961–
    Whitney Houston / by Jeff Savage.—1st ed.
       p. cm.—(Taking part books)
    Summary: A biography of the popular singer who has recorded such hits as
"The Greatest Love Of All" and "I Will Always Love You" and starred in such
movies as "The Bodyguard" and "Waiting to Exhale."
    ISBN 0-382-39797-5 (lsb.) —ISBN 0-382-39798-3 (scr)
    1. Houston, Whitney—Juvenile literature.   2. Singers—United States—
Biography—Juvenile literature. [1. Houston, Whitney. 2. Singers. 3. Afro-
Americans—Biography. 4. Women—Biography.]   I. Title.
ML3930.H7S28   1998
782.42164'092—dc21   97-2713
[B]

Cover and book design by Michelle Farinella

 Published by Dillon Press
A Division of Simon & Schuster
299 Jefferson Road, Parsippany, NJ 07054

First Edition

Printed in the United States of America
10 9 8 7 6 5 4 3 2 1

Contents

Whitney sings in a dramatic scene from The Bodyguard.

Introduction

Whitney Houston was at home playing Scrabble one day when the telephone rang. It was Kevin Costner. The Academy Award-winning actor and director was calling to ask Whitney to make a movie with him.

Whitney was then a pop singer whose towering, dynamic voice had made her a superstar. She had the best-selling debut album ever by a solo artist. She had surpassed Madonna at the top of the charts and had gone on to record more number-one hits in a row than the Beatles. She had become wealthy, with her own makeup artist and hairdresser and chauffeur, and she lived like a queen in her $11-million mansion in Mendham, New Jersey.

But acting? Whitney had never been an actor. She had worked briefly as a model for magazine covers, and she had even appeared once in a soap opera. But the movies? Hollywood? Whitney was nervous about the idea and told Costner so.

"I promised her two things," Costner told *Ebony* magazine in January 1993. "That I would be right there with her, and that she would not be bad, because I refuse to let anybody fail around me."

Costner even told Whitney that he could use some singing tips. Whitney finally agreed. She would help him with his singing if he would help her with the acting.

The movie was called *The Bodyguard*, and it turned out that Whitney did not need much help. Her performance was superb. She played the role of a superstar named Rachel, who was stalked by a crazy man. Costner played the bodyguard. The movie took three months to make. Although Whitney appeared calm as she read her lines and acted out her role, she admitted she was scared. "I wanted to do some acting, but I mean, I never thought I'd be costarring with Kevin Costner!" Whitney told *Ebony* magazine. "Acting requires a lot of concentration. I would compare it with starting my music career. It was like starting all over again, but in a new field."

The Bodyguard premiered on November 23, 1992, at the famous Mann's Chinese Theater in Hollywood. Critics loved it. The movie was released that week to the public and became an instant box-office hit. Around the world, people stood in long lines at theaters to see Whitney's first film. Within a year *The Bodyguard* had made more than $400 million worldwide. Whitney also sang six songs for

Whitney walks with Kevin Costner in The Bodyguard.

the movie, and the soundtrack sold 33 million copies. The emotional theme song "I Will Always Love You" zoomed to the top of the pop music charts and stayed there longer than any other song in history.

Whitney knew she was a great singer, but she still didn't really consider herself a movie star. "Now that I've done this one, and learned from it," she said in the April 1993 issue of *Ladies Home Journal*, "I want to try again sometime." That time would come sooner than she thought. Whitney didn't know it yet, but she was about to become one of the hottest female actors ever.

1

A Perfect
Little Lady

Whitney Houston grew up in a world of music. She was born August 9, 1963, in Newark, New Jersey, to Cissy and John Houston. Cissy was a member of the gospel and blues group the Drinkard Sisters, and she later sang backup to stars like Luther Vandross and Elvis Presley. John was a part-time singer who also worked in a city-government office. Whitney's cousin is pop star Dionne Warwick, and her godmother is soul queen Aretha Franklin.

As Cissy and John waited in the hospital a few hours before the birth of their last child, a sitcom called *Hazel* appeared on television. One of the actors on the show was a bright, classy, confident woman named Whitney Blake. Cissy decided right then that if the baby was a girl, her name would be Whitney.

Whitney grew up with her older brothers, Michael and Gary, in a small apartment in a poor area of Newark. As a young girl, she was always happy and smiling, unaware of the poverty around her. "Whitney was a big talker," her mother told *Ebony* magazine in the May 1995 issue. "She

All grown up, Whitney smiles as she performs for the audience.

Whitney enjoys the company of her cousin Dionne Warwick.

loved to talk . . . she was a delight to take anywhere. She was a perfect little lady."

When Whitney was four, the family packed up its belongings and moved several miles west to the suburb of East Orange. Cissy began singing background vocals for such big artists as Elvis Presley, Connie Francis, Buddy Rich, and Dusty Springfield. She also formed her own group, the Sweet Inspirations. Cissy's group toured with Aretha Franklin and spent countless hours in the recording studio. Whitney often went with her mother to the studio and would stand in the corner and hum along as her mother's group recorded songs. Sometimes Whitney would sing so loudly that Cissy would have to remove her from the studio. Aretha Franklin remembers Whitney's spirit as a child. "She wanted to sing," Aretha told Jeffrey Bowman, author of *Diva*. "I knew it even then. She'd say, 'I want to be a Sweet Inspiration, too.'"

Whitney's mother did not pressure her daughter to be a singer. In fact, she thought that Whitney would become a school teacher when she grew up. But Whitney had some painful experiences in school. In elementary school she always did her homework and made good grades, but she was teased cruelly by her classmates. She was taunted for having lighter skin than other African American

11

children. And while other kids wore shabby clothes to school, Whitney's mother dressed her daughter in frilly outfits with shiny shoes. "People just didn't like me," Whitney revealed in the May 1994 issue of *Cosmopolitan* magazine. "This was a time when black meant black power and Afros, and I was a light-skinned girl with long hair. Everybody else wore jeans and ripped sweatshirts, and there I was, standing out in skirts and sweaters."

Whitney sat at her desk in class and looked straight forward, trying to ignore the heartless whispering and teasing. At recess and lunchtime she sneaked behind classroom buildings so that no one could harass her. She hated hiding. Sometimes a group of jealous girls would spot her and come after her. They would tear her clothes and yank the ribbons from her hair. When she escaped, she would run home crying. But her mother would turn her around and send her right back to school. Kevin Ammons, author of *Good Girl, Bad Girl,* said Whitney's mother would tell her, "If you don't stand up for yourself and show them you're not afraid, they'll never leave you alone." Whitney sometimes had to stand and fight the other girls.

Music always put Whitney in a good mood. She especially liked the emotional singing of Aretha Franklin,

Aretha Franklin

whom she called Aunt Ree. In the family's basement at home, Whitney would play Aretha's records and sing along. She would hold her mother's microphone and wail out the lyrics as loudly as she could. Her parents could hear her from upstairs, and sometimes her father would grow annoyed with the noise. "Her father would say, 'Can't you do something about that girl, about that screaming?'" Cissy told *Ebony* magazine in May 1995. "And I would say, 'Maybe one day it will develop her voice.'"

When she was nine, Whitney joined the choir at the
New Hope Baptist Church, which the family attended.
It was here that she learned the key elements of singing.
"Gospel," Whitney said in the January 1996 issue of
Harper's Bazaar magazine, "taught me a wide range of
things: how to sing fast, how to sing slow, how to sing
when the tempo changes in the middle of a song, how to
sing four-part harmony without thinking about it. And
how to sing without music, in terms of your voice being
the instrument, your feet being the drum, your hands
being the tambourine."

After singing two years in the choir, Whitney believed
that she was ready for her first solo. She stood alone
before the congregation one Sunday morning ready to
sing "Guide Me, O Thou Great Jehovah." But when she
looked out and saw everyone staring at her, she became
terrified. "I was so afraid, so scared, that I closed my eyes
and just began to sing," she told *Essence Magazine* in
December 1990. Her voice was so sweet and filled with
emotion that the audience went wild. People jumped to
their feet and started clapping and stomping and shouting, and for a moment all the commotion frightened
Whitney. "When I opened my eyes, it was like the Holy
Spirit had come to the church. People were just shouting

The church that Whitney and her family attended in Newark, New Jersey

and happy and praising God." Whitney could hardly believe the effect her singing had on people. She made up her mind right then that she had to be a singer.

After sixth grade, Whitney enrolled in Mount St. Dominic Academy—a private school for girls. Her parents hoped that with a different set of schoolmates the teasing would stop. It didn't. Whitney had been lonely in elementary school, and now she was too bashful to make friends. She was pretty, with her buttery skin and warm brown eyes, and the other girls were jealous

15

of her. Whitney knew that she was beautiful, but she never showed it. According to a July 1991 issue of *People Weekly* magazine, Whitney had often been warned by her mother, "Pretty can turn into pretty awful if you act that way." Still, the other girls invented reasons not to like Whitney. She was shy, but they called her conceited. Because she had prim and proper manners, they called her prissy. School life for Whitney was miserable.

Another event brought her even more unhappiness. John and Cissy were divorced, and he moved out. Whitney and her father had always been close. He loved her and affectionately called her Nippy. She admired him almost as a hero. Now he was leaving the house. He would still see her often, but it wouldn't be the same. She felt abandoned and alone.

Whitney's mother stepped in to fill the void. She took time out from work to attend Whitney's school functions. She spent time with her daughter at night and on weekends. She went everywhere with Whitney. Once Whitney and her mother were strolling along Seventh Avenue in New York City when a man approached Whitney. He was a talent scout for a modeling agency. He handed Whitney his business card and asked her to stop by his office. Whitney went with her mother to

Whitney Houston with her parents at a press conference to promote the Special Olympics

the agency that day, and she was signed on the spot.

A month later Whitney's face appeared in the magazine *Mademoiselle*. Now her classmates were *really* jealous. Whitney tried not to let them bother her. She focused on her schoolwork and got A's and B's. She joined a larger modeling agency and soon was doing layouts for such notable magazines as *Cosmopolitan* and *Glamour*. Most girls would do backflips to be a model, but not Whitney. She quickly grew bored with modeling. What Whitney really wanted was to sing. She was about to get that chance.

CHAPTER

2

A Rising Star

Ever since that day in church when Whitney decided to be a singer, her mother had been coaching her. Whitney learned to control her voice—to let it rise and fall and flow with the music. In the recording studio she learned to work the sound board and dub sounds together. She began to sing with her mother in local clubs to gain experience in front of an audience. At 15 years old, she was already singing backup vocals with her mother for such artists as Lou Rawls and Chaka Khan.

Talented singer Luther Vandross heard Whitney's voice one day, and he immediately offered to produce Whitney's first album. Her parents said no. They thought that she was still too young to be a solo artist. They told her she had to finish high school first. The mere thought of two more years of school, surrounded by jealous girls, left Whitney feeling distressed.

Happily, Whitney had a friend now. Her mother had encouraged her to be a volunteer counselor at a summer camp for children, and there she met Robyn Crawford.

Long coached by her mother, Whitney has learned to control her voice and has gained experience performing for audiences.

Whitney Houston's best friend, Robyn Crawford, is seen here with Whitney's brother Michael.

Robyn, two years older, was pretty, too, and she was not jealous of Whitney at all. The two girls became close friends, sharing secrets and going everywhere together. They told people they were sisters and often wore identical clothes. Today they remain best friends, and Whitney calls Robyn "the sister I never had."

Whitney continued to model for such magazines as *Vogue* and *Harper's Bazaar.* "Where else could a kid make that kind of money for doing nothing?" she reflects. When she turned 17, she sang her first solo on Michael Zager's album *Life's a Party.* The producer was so impressed with her dynamic voice that he offered her a recording contract. Again her mother said no. Cissy knew that the entertainment world is competitive and filled with heartbreak, and she was merely trying to protect her daughter.

At last, in June 1981, Whitney graduated from Mount St. Dominic. Her grades were good enough for entering

most colleges, but Whitney
had no desire for more
schooling. Her future was
the music business—she
just *knew* it.

Immediately upon grad-
uation, Whitney signed
with a talent management
company called Tara
Productions. Her personal
manager, Gene Harvey, got
her singing parts on albums
by the Neville Brothers and
the funk band Material. She
sang "Eternal Love" on
another album, and people
in the music industry began
to take notice.

*Whitney and her mother share a happy
moment at Cissy's home in 1985.*

As Whitney and her mother performed at Manhattan's
nightclubs, word spread about this fresh new songbird
from New Jersey. Talent scouts began showing up to
see her perform. One night a manager from Elektra
Records met Whitney and her parents backstage and
offered her a recording contract. Elektra was a popular

Whitney (with tambourine) *performs as part of her mother's backup group.*

label, and John and Cissy were thrilled. Whitney was so excited she nearly fainted.

As Gene Harvey and executives at Elektra began to negotiate a contract, Whitney continued her nightclub performances. One evening at a supper club in Greenwich Village, Whitney learned that talent scout Gerry Griffith was in the audience. Griffith was an assistant for Clive Davis, one of the greatest talent managers ever. Davis managed such artists as Bob Dylan, Janis

Joplin, Barry Manilow, and Santana. Davis had been the president of CBS Records for many years, but now he owned his own label, Arista Records. Whitney gave an inspiring performance that night, and Griffith convinced her afterward to do an audition for Davis. Whitney had not yet signed a deal with Elektra, and so she agreed.

Whitney's audition for Clive Davis was held at Top Hat Rehearsal Hall in Manhattan. Whitney may have been nervous, but you never would have known it. She overwhelmed Davis with her beautiful voice and her energetic stage presence. When Davis offered Whitney an album contract, she didn't have to think twice. Elektra was out; Arista and Clive Davis were in. Whitney was about to become a star.

Clive Davis worked carefully with Whitney. He assembled a team of songwriters and producers to create songs just for her. Then he arranged for her to appear on *The Merv Griffin Show* in Hollywood. Davis selected an ordinary skirt-and-sweater outfit for Whitney to wear, to give her the appearance of an innocent schoolgirl. But when the spotlight was on her, Whitney was anything but shy. She dazzled the audience and television viewers nationwide with a dynamic rendition of the song "Home."

Davis then arranged for Whitney to sing duets with

Teddy Pendergrass and Jermaine Jackson on their newest albums. Both albums sold well, and the public wanted to hear more of Whitney. The time had finally come for her to record her own album.

Davis arranged the material for Whitney's debut album, and for the next four months, she worked hard in the recording studio, making each song perfect. When the album was finished, Davis released it one song at a time. He used MTV to showcase her beauty along with her voice, starting with "You Give Good Love" in which Whitney stood and sang directly into the camera. This music video was followed by "Saving All My Love for You," "The Greatest Love of All," and finally the jazzy tune "How Will I Know?" in which Whitney skipped and swayed among a stageful of professional dancers.

In February 1985, Whitney's debut album, *Whitney Houston,* was released. The public went crazy over it. Across the country, millions of children and adults of all ages flocked to record stores to buy the album. Whitney's head was spinning. Could she really be this popular so quickly? To help boost sales further, Whitney embarked in June on a five-month tour of the United States. She hated to leave her family and her cat, Misty Blue, but she understood the importance of promoting her music. The tour zigzagged across the Midwest and then through the South, with Whitney's popularity rising every day. She was paid $15,000 per show when the tour began, but her fame grew so quickly that by August she was earning $100,000 a show. The tour finally ended in November with a series of sold-out performances at New York's Carnegie Hall, where a *New York Times* music reviewer compared Whitney's voice to that of "an Olympic athlete."

By then Whitney's debut album had sold 6 million copies in the United States and was still going strong. Its total sales of 10 million worldwide had surpassed all other first-time female artists except Madonna. Whitney was stunned by her instant success.

Fabulous surprises continued in early 1986 as Whitney's name was announced among the nominees for the 28th annual Grammy Awards. Whitney sat in the audience with her parents as her cousin Dionne Warwick walked on stage to present the award for Best Female Pop Performance. Dionne nervously opened the envelope and read the winning name: Whitney Houston. Dionne shrieked with delight and twirled in a circle as she screamed Whitney's name. Now it was Whitney's turn to scream. She hurried to the stage amid the roars

After accepting her first Grammy Award, Whitney beams with happiness.

of the crowd and hugged her cousin as she accepted the award trophy. She stood at the microphone, beaming, thanked God and her parents, and said, "I feel just like Cinderella!"

Whitney's first two singles releases, "You Give Good Love" and "Saving All My Love for You," were already hovering near the top of the charts when "How Will I Know?" shot past them in March to hit number one on *Billboard* magazine's pop singles chart. "The Greatest Love of All" followed later in the spring to the top spot. From March to June, Whitney's album held at the number one spot, the longest streak in 16 years. By then it had sold more than 18 million copies, making it the biggest-selling debut album ever by a solo artist. "Who's buying it?" Whitney cried, according to Kevin Ammons, author of *Good Girl, Bad Girl*. "I thought everybody in the world had one by now!"

At this time Whitney also discovered another side of the entertainment business—the critics. Some claimed that her music was too simple and bland. Others complained that because she is African American, she ought to be singing strictly for African American tastes rather than everybody. Whitney did not understand all the fuss. "What is 'Black'?" she asked in *Essence Magazine*'s

December 1990 issue. "I don't know how to sing 'Black,' and I don't know how to sing 'White,' either. I know how to sing. Music is not a color to me. It's an art." Her mother came to her defense as well. "What is the problem with crossover, anyway?" Cissy asked. "It's the only way you can reach your public."

While the critics argued over what was best for Whitney, she was busy enjoying her new-found fame. On the Fourth of July, she sang "The Greatest Love of All" on national television for the Statue of Liberty's centennial celebration. Then she and her parents were honored by the mayor of Newark, New Jersey, and she was presented with the highest tribute any city can bestow—a key to the city. What did all her former schoolmates think of Whitney now? She was the toast of the town. She was a shooting star.

3

Breaking Records and Winning Awards

Whitney had become a millionaire. Everything had happened so fast that it all seemed a blur. Suddenly she found herself on the cover of magazines, riding in limousines, dining in fine restaurants, and staying in elegant hotels. She had a team of assistants, even a personal hair stylist. Clive Davis made all the major decisions for her career, but her father became her manager, her mother acted as her adviser, and her brothers, Gary and Michael, served as bodyguards. Even her best friend, Robyn Crawford, was hired as a personal executive. They were all paid well for their services.

Whitney returned to the recording studio early in 1986 to work on her second album. Her team of songwriters had prepared a whole new set of songs for her to perform. She spent several months in the sound booth, singing each song dozens of times and polishing every note. Her first album was still selling briskly, so there was no reason to release this second album right away.

In August, after Whitney had put all she could of her

Now famous, Whitney has become a hero to children.

voice into the studio recordings, it was up to the producers to splice the sounds together and make the music perfect, as in the first album. In the meantime, Whitney started a second tour of the United States. The tour began in Long Island, New York, where a reporter from *Newsday* described her as "silky-smooth and slinky-fast . . . her body a graceful, spikey motion machine." The shows for this second tour were staged in bigger arenas than the first, but the public was crazy for Whitney, and all her events sold out.

Whitney returned home to New Jersey four months later to more good news. She had been nominated once again for a Grammy Award for Best Female Pop Performance. And, once again, she won. It looked like 1987 would be another year to celebrate.

Whitney's second album was released to the public in June. It was titled simply *Whitney*. By now everyone knew her by her first name anyway. The moment the album was released, it was listed number one on the pop charts. Whitney was the only female artist ever to have her album become number one the same day it was released.

Whitney's high-energy tunes "I Wanna Dance with Somebody" and "So Emotional" immediately shot to the top of the singles charts, as did "Where Do Broken

31

Performing "I Wanna Dance with Somebody" at Madison Square Garden, Whitney wows her audience.

Hearts Go?" and "Love Will Save the Day." With these four number-one hits from her second album, combined with three number ones from her first, Whitney set an amazing record. She became the first musician in history to have seven consecutive number-one songs. She broke the mark previously held by the Bee Gees and the Beatles. Once again, millions of people were flocking to the record stores to buy the hot album by superstar Whitney Houston.

Whitney earned an incredible $44 million in 1987. Only Madonna earned more with $47 million. She was fabulously rich! Whitney bought fine houses for her parents, and then she bought one for herself on a five-acre estate in Mendham, New Jersey. The mansion is made mostly of glass and chrome and is worth $11 million. It has huge circular rooms, a recording studio, and an outdoor Olympic-sized pool.

Whitney had to pay another price for such luxury. She was now a famous public figure. The quiet private life she once had was over. Fans everywhere wanted to know the latest gossip about Whitney, and so the press followed her every move. Whitney had difficulty adjusting to it. "I make records that people will, I think, enjoy," she told *Harper's Bazaar* magazine in January 1996, "and that obviously isn't enough as far as the press is concerned."

Whitney still managed to enjoy some private times, like watching TV, playing backgammon or the card game spades, and talking on the telephone, sometimes for hours at a time, with her friend Robyn Crawford. Her mother's lifelong friend, "Aunt Bae," cooked most of her meals, and Whitney enjoyed her favorite foods like candied yams, fried chicken, and baked macaroni and cheese. But whenever Whitney stepped outside her mansion, she was surrounded by TV cameras, photographers, and fans wanting her autograph. It got so bad that bodyguards had to be stationed outside her house. She even needed a bodyguard with her when she shopped at the supermarket. "Whitney is a normal person who likes to do normal things and would like to lead a normal life," her mother said in the May 1995 issue of *Redbook* magazine. "But of course, she can't."

Whitney continued to win awards for her music. At the 1988 American Music Awards, she won two, including one for the song "I Wanna Dance with Somebody." But some people were still criticizing her for not singing African American styles of music. When her name was announced at the 1989 Soul Train Music Awards as the winner for Best Album by a Female Vocalist, many in the

Smiling broadly, Whitney displays her two 1988 American Music Awards.

crowd booed. Whitney was hurt by the booing as she walked to the stage to receive her award. Clive Davis was even more upset. He decided that Whitney's third album should have more rhythm-and-blues songs to please everyone.

As Whitney returned to her seat in the audience, a young man on the stage began performing a showy number that got the crowd buzzing. He was Bobby Brown, an energetic performer who was fast becoming a superstar himself. Bobby had grown up in the dangerous Roxbury neighborhood of Boston, Massachusetts, and he had a reputation for being street-tough. When Whitney met him backstage after the awards show, she liked him instantly. Bobby was only 22 years old, five years younger than Whitney, but it didn't matter to either of them, and they began dating.

Whitney returned to the recording studio to make her third album, but she also made a point to spend time working for good causes and to share her wealth. She formed The Whitney Houston Foundation for Children, Inc., an organization that helps children who are homeless or have cancer or AIDS. She established the Whitney Houston Pediatric Special Care Unit at a hospital in Newark, New Jersey, which provides vital care for

Clive Davis (left) *with Quincy Jones, Whitney Houston, Bobby Brown, and Bonnie Raitt at a pre-Grammy party*

seriously ill children. She began performing at a number of benefits to raise money for such causes as the United Negro College Fund and at tributes to great artists such as Sammy Davis, Jr.

Clive Davis made sure that Whitney's third album had a harder edge to it. On the album cover, Whitney sat on a Harley-Davidson motorcycle, trying to look tough. Inside, the music was up-tempo, with rhythmic pieces, soulful ballads, and energetic dance tracks. It was titled

Whitney sings "The Star-Spangled Banner" to honor the troops returning from the Persian Gulf War.

I'm Your Baby Tonight and was released in September 1990. While this album didn't sell like Whitney's first two, it still broke several sales records.

By now Whitney had become friendly with other superstars like singer Hammer, actor Eddie Murphy, and quarterback Randall Cunningham. She was living the fast life, riding around in her Jeep or her purple limousine and signing autographs everywhere she went. The Whitney Houston craze was still sweeping the country.

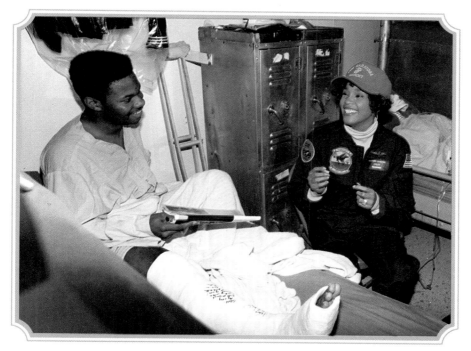

*Whitney visits with an injured
sailor aboard the U.S.S.* Saratoga.

In January 1991, Whitney was asked to perform the national anthem at the Super Bowl in Tampa, Florida. It was a time of national pride in the country because American troops were involved in the Persian Gulf War. Whitney gave a stirring rendition of the anthem to the delight of the crowd and a worldwide television audience of over 100 million viewers. Then she settled into her sky-box seat with her friends Hammer and Robyn Crawford to watch the game between the New York Giants and

Buffalo Bills. She didn't know at the time that her song would be made into a single and that it would soar to the top of the charts. Later, when she learned that millions of people had bought the single, she humbly told *Harper's Bazaar* magazine in January 1996, "My timing was right with it." Then she donated more than half a million dollars from sales to the American Red Cross Gulf Crisis Fund.

In 1991 when Kevin Costner asked Whitney to appear in a movie with him, she realized her career was about to blossom in a new direction. Costner had directed and starred in *Dances With Wolves,* which won seven Academy Awards. He was certainly capable of launching her career in the movies. Whitney's boyfriend, Bobby Brown, had appeared in a movie himself, *Ghostbusters II,* and he encouraged Whitney to try acting. Whitney agreed and left for Miami, Florida, to start the filming. Bobby stayed behind but called every day, and once even sent her 400 roses.

Whitney performed her acting role well, but not every moment was easy. In one particularly difficult scene, Whitney was supposed to angrily confront Costner and then slap him. The acting required a lot of emotion, and Whitney had to do several takes before she got it right. "I had to slap him several times," she told *Ebony* magazine in January 1993. "I kept saying, 'Oh, God, I don't want to hit this man because this man didn't do anything to me.' And I had to really slap him hard. That was very difficult."

One night Bobby Brown flew in to see Whitney. When they got into the car at the airport parking lot, Bobby reached into his pockets and nervously fumbled around looking for something. He pulled out a ring with a tiny diamond and showed it to Whitney. "It was really cute," Whitney recalled in the July 1994 issue of *Ebony* magazine. "I [thought], 'I'm in love with this man and he's going to ask me to marry him. I don't care about the ring.'" Bobby shyly looked up at Whitney and said, "Will you marry me?" Whitney screamed with joy. "Yes!" she cried. Then Bobby reached into his other pocket and pulled out another ring. "This is the real one," he said. "I just wanted to see how you would react." Bobby handed Whitney a gold ring with a huge ten-carat diamond. Whitney was stunned. "He played me like I was Atari," she told *Ebony*. "He tested my nerve. This ring blew my mind." Whitney tingled with excitement. She threw her arms around Bobby and cried. She was about to be married.

Whitney married Bobby Brown in a garden ceremony.

4

On to Hollywood

On July 18, 1992, just after 2 P.M., Whitney slipped into her gorgeous $40,000 wedding gown of white French lace, pearls, and beads. It covered her neck and shoulders, then dropped to the floor and flared out in a four-foot train of lace. She looked beautiful as she giggled with her maid of honor, Robyn Crawford, and her bridesmaids, all of them dressed in full-length purple dresses—Whitney's favorite color.

An hour later, in the garden gazebo behind Whitney's estate, the wedding ceremony began. Whitney walked down the aisle to the gazebo where Bobby was waiting. He was dressed handsomely in a white tuxedo with a silver jewel at the neck. Eight hundred guests watched happily as Whitney and Bobby exchanged vows. Among the guests were celebrities like Cosby kid Malcolm-Jamal Warner; Keenan Ivory Wayans from the TV show *In Living Color*; Robin Leach of *Lifestyles of the Rich and Famous*; basketball star Isiah Thomas; pop entertainer Dick Clark; and singers Gloria Estefan, Patti LaBelle,

Stevie Wonder, Gladys Knight, and Natalie Cole. As soon as the minister declared them husband and wife, Whitney and Bobby kissed, and seven white doves were released overhead.

The reception was held in an air-conditioned, carpeted ballroom tent on the estate. Thousands of lilacs and purple orchids lined the walls, turning the ballroom into something like an Arabian palace. The reception cost $1 million. As guests departed, they were given gift bags containing a bottle of champagne, a slice of wedding cake, and a note: "Place this cake under your pillow and dream of your own true love."

The next day the couple flew on the Concorde to Europe where a luxurious 140-foot yacht was waiting to take them on a 10-day Mediterranean honeymoon cruise. The yacht was equipped with a crew of nine, along with a TV, VCR, stereo, and jacuzzi, and was paid for by Arista Records. The company could afford to spend money on its star performer, especially since it was about to make millions from another of Whitney's albums.

When Whitney returned to New Jersey with Bobby, the soundtrack to her movie, *The Bodyguard*, had just been released. It was an instant hit. The soundtrack included the six songs from the movie along with several

Whitney performs at the Kids' Choice Awards show in Universal City, California.

other songs by Whitney, and swarms of people poured into record stores to buy it. Oprah Winfrey loved the song "I'm Every Woman" so much that she used it as the theme song for her television show. But the biggest hit of all was "I Will Always Love You," with Whitney singing the familiar strain "I-ee-I-ee-I" in her sweet voice.

As the months went by and sales for the soundtrack grew, so did Whitney. She and Bobby were expecting their first baby in the spring. Because she was pregnant, Whitney had to reschedule the concert tour to promote

*Expectant mother Whitney with
husband Bobby Brown*

the soundtrack. It didn't seem to matter, as sales continued to soar. The movie was released late in 1992, and it
swept the country, too. By the time the excitement died
down, *The Bodyguard* had made nearly half a billion
dollars, and the soundtrack had sold a staggering
33 million copies worldwide.

Meanwhile, Whitney had gained 50 pounds. On
March 4, 1993, she gave birth to a baby girl. Whitney
and Bobby named her Bobbi Kristina Houston Brown.

Whitney was elated to have a child, but now she had to get back in shape for the soundtrack concert tour. She rehearsed six hours a day, swam a lot, and did stomach crunches. Eventually she returned to her original weight of 122 pounds on her 5-foot-8-inch frame. The tour began in August.

Life on the road is never easy for a performer, and it was especially draining for Whitney this time. Bobby traveled with her for much of the tour, and she was always making sure he was comfortable. They also brought along little Bobbi Kristina, and Whitney often worried about her, even though Cissy was along to help.

To make matters worse, two stalkers were following Whitney. One had been sending her flowers almost weekly. Police had put him in jail for two months when they found several illegal weapons, including a crossbow, in his truck. But now he was on the loose again. The other had written letters threatening to visit her, and he even moved to Newark, New Jersey, to be near her. It seemed that Whitney was safe with her bodyguards surrounding her, just like in her movie, but in the back of her mind she wondered if it was enough.

Whitney also had to bail out Bobby from tax troubles. He had fallen behind on payments for the $1.5 million mansion in Atlanta, Georgia, that he owned before he met Whitney. The government had seized control of the house. But Whitney's management company, Nippy, Inc., bought it back for Bobby.

When the exhausting tour finally ended, Whitney had to deal with the whispers that her marriage to Bobby was about to fail. Bobby had gotten mixed up in a few scuffles, and some reporters were writing that Whitney was ready to leave him. Whitney denounced these stories as vicious rumors.

Whitney's frustration with the press grew, especially with tabloids, which often stretch the truth. One reporter even stupidly asked Whitney, "Will you ever get married again?" She snapped that she already was married. "The media overkill is so draining," she explained later in the July 1994 issue of *Ebony* magazine. "We have a regular marriage like everybody else. It bothers us that they say things so horrible and negative about a person that are totally untrue."

Whitney had always been fair with the press. She couldn't understand why they seemed to pick on her. She even invited reporters into her mansion in Mendham for interviews and then made them sandwiches for their drive back to New York. Kevin Costner told *Redbook* magazine in May 1995, "As popular as Whitney is, she takes [unfair] shots from the media. She is a real big target."

Whitney's mother had tried to protect Whitney from the dark side of a celebrity's world. Cissy had long known this side existed. Fans see their favorite celebrities on the stage or the movie screen, but they don't see the constant hounding that celebrities have to endure. With her mother's guidance, Whitney handled the press as best she could.

Whitney and Bobby celebrated their first anniversary quietly at home. They set up a table in the back yard, covered it with their wedding tablecloth, and lit some candles. They ate dinner and wedding cake and then danced under the stars. On her 30th birthday, Whitney was performing in France when Bobby surprised her by throwing a party for her on a yacht anchored in the Mediterranean. It reminded them both of their honeymoon a year earlier.

Whitney was in for another surprise at the American Music Awards in February 1994. She was seated in the audience at the Shrine Auditorium in Los Angeles with husband Bobby, daughter Bobbi Kris, and her parents, when her name was announced for an award for the soundtrack from *The Bodyguard*. She took the stage with her husband and daughter and thanked everyone, with little Bobbi in her arms grabbing at the microphone to the delight of the crowd. Whitney returned to her seat, only to hear her name called again. This time she went up alone and gratefully accepted her second award. Then her name was announced a third time. Then a fourth. Then a fifth. Before the night was over, Whitney had set a record by winning eight American Music Awards in a single year. She also tied Kenny Rogers for most in a lifetime with 19.

The honors continued for Whitney a month later at the Grammy Awards. She won three times—for Top Female Vocalist, Album of the Year, and Song of the Year. "I want to thank everybody who bought the record, who loved it," Whitney said onstage. "God bless you. Peace." When newcomer Toni Braxton won for best rhythm-and-blues female artist, she was surprised that Whitney didn't win that award, too. "I can't believe it," Braxton announced. "I mean, Whitney is my favorite."

In the following months, Whitney kept busy by performing at a rain forest benefit with Sting at Carnegie Hall, going on a world tour in which she appeared

Whitney and South Africa's Deputy Minister of Arts and Culture, Winnie Mandela, are welcomed to a children's home outside Capetown, South Africa.

before crowds of 50,000 and more, and hosting a concert in Johannesburg, South Africa, that was broadcast live on HBO. Whitney donated all proceeds from that concert to a children's group. She remained in Johannesburg for three weeks to walk through the neighborhoods and meet the residents. Before leaving she met South African president Nelson Mandela. She met Mandela again in the fall at the White House when she performed in the East Room for President Clinton and his guests.

Whitney admitted that her whirlwind life was tiring her out. Instead of taking a break, however, she revved up her acting career. Ever since *The Bodyguard* had become a smash hit, she was flooded with requests by movie companies. She read several scripts but couldn't find one that suited her—until now. Acclaimed actor Forest Whitaker was about to direct a movie about four African American women who search for good, honest men. The movie would be called *Waiting to Exhale* and be based on the book by author Terry McMillan. "I loved the characters in the book," Whitney said in *Essence* magazine in December 1995, "and I always loved Forest Whitaker's work." Whitney couldn't refuse.

Filming started in the spring of 1995 on location in Arizona. Whitney was inspired to be working with actors Angela Bassett, Loretta Devine, and Lela Rochon. She remembered when she was 15 meeting Devine backstage at a club in New York. And everyone was just as thrilled to work with Whitney, too. "Everyone got along," author McMillan told *Harper's Bazaar* magazine in January 1996. "They'd be sitting there giggling and carrying on—you'd swear they'd known each other for years."

Whitney played the role of an ambitious woman named Savannah, who moves to Phoenix to pursue a career as a TV producer. Forest Whitaker had told her not to take acting lessons because he wanted her just to be natural. Whitney rose at 6:00 A.M. each morning with the rest of the cast and often worked late into the night. In one scene, Angela, Lela, and Whitney are supposed to sing "Happy Birthday" to Loretta. But Angela and Lela were too embarrassed to sing with Whitney. At first they just wanted to mouth the words. But with some persuading, the other two women joined Whitney in the song.

The film took ten weeks to make. Whitney also sang several songs for the movie's soundtrack. When her work was finished, she returned home to New Jersey for a long rest. She finally got to spend quality time with young Bobbi Kris. "I've never found anything more fulfilling than being a mother," she told *Ebony* magazine in May 1995. "Bobbi Kristina is our jewel. She is my whole life now."

Waiting to Exhale opened in theaters December 22, 1995, and instantly became a hit. Women clapped and cheered all through the movie, identifying themselves

Denzel Washington with Whitney in
a scene from The Preacher's Wife

with the characters on the screen. Critics called the acting superb, and many singled out Whitney for her beauty and brilliance.

When Whitney said that she would like to do yet another film, she was flooded with scripts. Nearly every motion-picture company in the United States begged her to sign with them. The highest-paid female actors in 1996 were Demi Moore, Julia Roberts, and Sandra

Little Bobbi Kristina and mom Whitney
arrive at the premiere of The Preacher's Wife.

Bullock, with salaries of $10 million per film. When Whitney signed a contract in 1996 to do *The Preacher's Wife,* a movie about an angel who helps a preacher build a church, she joined them. Whitney's asking price to appear in the film was $10 million. She got it. She might have gotten even more had she asked for it. As it is, she is now one of the most sought-after and best-paid female actors ever.

CHAPTER

5

Caring and Sharing

Whitney Houston enjoys a comfortable life. She rides around in a new black Rolls-Royce limousine. When she feels like getting away, she can go to her home in North Miami Beach or her other home in the Caribbean.

But Whitney is also generous. She shares her wealth in many ways. She works with St. Jude's Children's Hospital, The Children's Diabetes Fund, and many other children's organizations. Through the Whitney Houston Foundation for Children, she hopes to fight illiteracy. "When you can't read, you don't understand," she told a reporter for *Essence* magazine in December 1990. "That worries me about people in America."

When Whitney gives a concert, sometimes she keeps the money made from ticket sales for her family. Other times she uses the money to pay her staff of assistants. Still other times she gives the money to charity. When she does, it usually goes to a children's group. To Whitney, children are more important than anything else.

A concert by Whitney will always sell out, no matter

Whitney celebrates with President and Mrs. George Bush as the Olympic flag arrives in Atlanta.

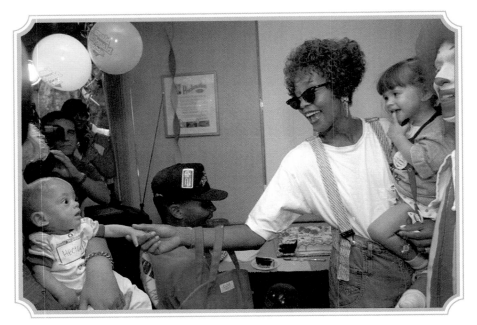

*Before a Miami concert, Whitney takes time to visit
seriously ill children at the Ronald McDonald House.*

what. People fill arenas and concert halls and stadiums
to see her wherever she goes. She has sold more than
100 million albums worldwide and is the top female
music award winner of all time. She is a shining star
among singers.

Now she can be counted among the great Hollywood
actors, too. When *The Preacher's Wife,* also starring
Denzel Washington and Courtney B. Vance, was released
in December 1996, crowds swarmed to theaters to see
Whitney again. For the third straight time, she had starred

*Whitney and Denzel Washington
host the NAACP Image Awards
in Pasadena, California.*

in a popular movie. In 1997 Whitney began work on two more films—one about actress Dorothy Dandridge, the other a TV movie in which she played Cinderella's fairy godmother.

Whitney has learned some hard lessons on her way to fame. She admits the road hasn't always been smooth. "You can't really plan fame or what you'll do with it once you have it," she said in *Redbook* magazine's May 1995 issue. "Or how you'll handle it. Or how you'll feel about your audiences. Or how they'll feel about you. But through all the madness and the peaks and the cooldowns, I've maintained my basic values."

Whitney Houston would never trade her life for anyone else's. She would rather be the one getting teased in school than the one doing the teasing. She knows that people who tease usually don't get too far in life. But Whitney has gone far; she has gone as far in the entertainment business as anyone. And she has a message to tell the world. The message, as she told *Ladies Home Journal* magazine in April 1993, is this: "Tell them that Whitney Houston still loves entertaining as much as she did when she was nineteen. And she probably still will when she's ninety-nine."

Whitney Houston loves to entertain audiences.

Index

About the Author

Jeff Savage is the author of over 60 books for young adults. When he isn't writing, he's probably reading, flying an airplane, practicing karate, or spending time with his wife, Nancy, and son, Taylor, in Napa, California.